THE CHRISTIAN

MW01000601

TEN BASIC STEPS TOWARD CHRISTIAN MATURITY — STEP 3

FOREWORD

by Bill Bright

The greatest spiritual awakening of all time is taking place today. More people are hearing the gospel, more are receiving Christ and more are committed to helping fulfill the Great Commission than at any other time since the church was born almost 2,000 years ago. Here in the United States, one-third of all adults identify themselves as born-again, evangelical Christians. Millions of people attend church regularly and listen to Christian radio and television programs.

But we have a serious problem — these facts are not reflected in the life of our nation. What has gone wrong?

According to statistics compiled as a result of surveys we have taken, more than 50% of the church members in America are not sure of their salvation (in some churches that figure might be 5%; in others, 95% depending on the denomination and the leadership of the church); 95% do not understand the ministry of the Holy Spirit; and 98% are not regularly sharing their faith in Christ.

Our Lord has commanded us to be the salt of the earth and the light of the world, but we see little evidence of the influence of Christianity. To effectively influence the world or his own community for Christ, a Christian must be growing spiritually, introducing men and women to the Savior and helping other believers reach a higher level of Christian maturity. An indepth study of God's Word is a major factor in accomplishing these things.

It is for this purpose the *Ten Basic Steps Toward Christian Maturity* course has been written. Designed originally to stimulate college students to explore the riches of God's Word, the course has been equally effective with adults and young people in churches, home Bible study groups, military and prison facilities and in many high schools.

Now, the entire work, including the *Ten Basic Steps Toward Christian Maturity Teacher's Manual,* has been revised and updated, and is as useful by the individual Christian in his private Bible study, aiding him in his personal spiritual growth.

When used with the new Teacher's Manual, the revised series will be even more effective in a group situation, and is so prepared that even inexperienced, first-time teachers can lead and teach the Bible studies successfully. The lesson material in the booklets also has been combined in a single paperback volume called *A Handbook for Christian Maturity.,*

Our prayer is that these studies will bless and enrich your life, and that you will be further encouraged in your growth toward maturity in Jesus Christ. We trust also that the effectiveness of your personal witness for Him will be greatly enhanced.

INTRODUCTION

Inquisitive, intellectually minded, concerned people investigate a great many things to varying degrees, but frequently give little thought and even less time to Bible study. Yet the Bible undoubtedly has had a more profound effect on history than any other book. It has played a major part in the development of western culture, influencing national and international affairs as well as matters of everyday life. For any individual to be properly informed and well-educated, he must have at least a general knowledge of the Bible and its teachings. That knowledge can be acquired only through a consistent plan of study.

This *Ten Basic Steps Toward Christian Maturity* course is designed to give you an efficient means for a systematic study of the Christian faith as taught in the Bible. The benefit from your study should be two-fold:

First, a communication of knowledge. Without at least some Biblical teaching no one can become a Christian, and no Christian can live a victorious life. A great many people reject Christianity and a great many Christians are defeated and frustrated simply because of ignorance. The psalmist said, "The entrance of Thy Words giveth light" (Psalm 119:130), and Jesus taught that "the truth shall make you free" (John 8:32).

Second, power in your life. Hebrews 4:12 says, "The Word of God is quick and powerful, and sharper than any two-edged sword . . . and is a discerner of the thoughts and intents of the heart." Men and women by the thousands, including Augustine, Luther, Wesley and many others, have changed history because God used the Bible to change them.

As you begin to use this study, you undoubtedly will sense changes coming over you, too. You will be shown how to receive Christ as your Savior and will be given an opportunity to invite Him into your life if you have not already done so.

If you are a new Christian, you will begin to gain a knowledge of the Bible, becoming acquainted with the major doctrines of the Christian faith. You will grow spiritually and find some solutions to problems you may be facing.

If you are an older, more mature Christian, you will acquire the tools needed to help others find Christ and to help weak Christians grow in faith. Your own commitment will be affirmed and you will develop an effective devotional and study plan.

A faithful study of *Ten Basic Steps Toward Christian Maturity* will also show you the way to continual appropriation of the power of the Holy Spirit, enabling you to live a more joyous, triumphant Christian life.

INSTRUCTIONS
FOR INDIVIDUAL STUDY OF
TEN BASIC STEPS
TOWARD CHRISTIAN MATURITY

This course of study is designed to give you a broad survey of Christianity. You will meet its central figure, Jesus Christ, and you will study its authoritative literature, the Holy Bible. You will learn of the nature, privileges and responsibilities of Christian living, and you will discover the secret of its power to transform men and give them a continually abundant life.

The study is divided into 11 parts or steps, with an individual booklet for the introductory study and one for each of the ten steps. These booklets correlate closely with the *Handbook for Christian Maturity* and the revised *Ten Basic Steps Toward Christian Maturity Teacher's Manual*.

This study has been formulated to help you become established and mature in your relationship with Christ. Each Step reveals a different facet of Christian life and truth and contains lessons for daily study.

SUMMARY OF THIS STEP

Step 3: The Christian and the Holy Spirit

Step 3 is a discussion of the Holy Spirit, who is the third member of the Godhead, or Trinity. This Step teaches us who the Holy Spirit is and how He works in the lives of individuals. It shows us how we may have Him working in our own lives and what the results can be. It teaches us how we may have His power continually energizing us.

ORGANIZATION OF THE STUDIES

In the opening pages of this Step you will find the preparatory article, "You Shall Receive Power." Read it through carefully before proceeding with the individual studies. It will give you a clearer perspective on the subject.

There are six lessons plus a review or "Recap" lesson in this Step. Each lesson is divided into three sections, the Introduction, the Bible Study, and the Life Application.

The Introduction is comprised of the stated Objective for that lesson, a Scripture verse or two to memorize and appropriate Bible reading. The main goal for each lesson, the Objective, should be kept in mind as you continue through the lesson.

Memorizing the key verses of Scripture is one of the most effective ways to assimilate the Word of God as an aid to your Christian growth. Read the Scripture passages suggested. Some will be for general reading, others will be about the topic to be studied. As you read you will become acquainted with many important portions of the Bible. Select your favorite verse from this reading and add it to the verses already listed to be memorized.

Casual Bible reading uncovers valuable spiritual facts that lie near the surface. But to understand the deeper truths requires study. Often the difference between reading and study is a pen. Every lesson in this series contains a study of an important topic with an opportunity for you to record your answers to the questions. We recommend that you spend a minimum of 30 minutes each day, preferably in the morning, in Bible study, meditation and prayer.

MEMORIZATION

The memory verses have been provided to help you in your walk with Christ. As you study, you will find that by "binding certain truths on the table of your heart" you will be enabled to meet each situation as it arises. "Wherewithal shall a young man cleanse his way? By taking heed thereto according to Thy Word" (Psalm 119:9).

It is suggested that you learn each verse in connection with the corresponding lesson by writing it out on a small card. Cards for memorization can be obtained from any bookstore or print-shop or they can be made by cutting down filing cards. Retain the verses by reviewing daily.

The importance of memorizing as a means of study cannot be overemphasized. The Lord has commanded that we learn His Word. Proverbs 7:1-3 says, "My son, keep my words, and lay up my commandments with thee. Keep my commandments and live; and my law as the apple of thine eye. Bind them upon thy fingers, write them upon the table of thine heart."

As you memorize, you will experience some of the joy, victory and power which the memorized Word gives to the Christian's walk. Strive diligently to finish all the studies in the entire series and later, as you develop your own Bible study, continue to have a systematic method of memorization of God's Word.

HOW TO STUDY THE LESSONS

Plan a specific time and place in which to work on these studies. Make an appointment with God, then keep it.

Be sure you have a pen or pencil and your Bible along with this booklet.

Begin with prayer for God's wisdom.

Read over the entire lesson.

Meditate on the Objective to determine how it will fit into your particular circumstances or life.

Commit the suggested verse or verses to memory.

Read the suggested Scripture passages.

Proceed to the Bible Study, trusting God to use it to teach you. Work carefully and prayerfully, thinking through the questions, answering each as completely as possible.

When you come to the Life Application section, be honest with yourself as you answer the questions and apply them to your own life.

Continuing in an attitude of prayer, read through the lesson again and re-evaluate your Life Application answers. Do they need changing? Or adjusting? Review the memory work. Consider the Objective again and determine if it has been accomplished. If not, what do you need to do?

Close with a prayer of thanksgiving, commitment, surrender, or whatever is necessary to bring you to the point of growth which God has specifically revealed to you.

When you complete the Step, spend a little extra time on the Recap to make sure you understand every lesson thoroughly. If you don't, go back, ask God for wisdom again and go through whatever lesson(s) you need, until you do understand and are able to appropriate the truths for yourself.

These studies are not intended as a complete development of Christian beliefs. However, a careful study of the material will give you, with God's help, a sufficient understanding of how you may know and appropriate God's plan for your life. If fully absorbed, the spiritual truths contained here will assure you of the full and abundant life which Jesus promised in John 10:10.

The rate of speed with which you complete the studies is entirely up to you, but we encourage you not to go too fast. Give yourself time to think about the lessons, meditate on them and absorb the truths presented. Allow them to become a part of your life. Spend time in prayer with your Lord and enjoy His presence. Give God a chance to speak to you, and let the Holy Spirit teach you.

The Christian and the Holy Spirit

Be sure to read this article before beginning the lessons about the Holy Spirit.

YOU SHALL RECEIVE POWER

by Bill Bright

Has it ever occurred to you that there could be much more to the Christian life than what you are now experiencing?

Jesus said, "I came that they (you and I and all Christians) might have life, and might have it abundantly" (John 10:10). Yet, if you are an average professing Christian, you are undoubtedly thinking, "There is certainly nothing abundant about my life. I try to witness, but no one is interested in what I have to say. I experience nothing but doubts, fears, frustrations and defeat. Surely there must be something more to this Christian life, but I have never found it."

Because of the evangelistic emphasis of Campus Crusade, we have found it absolutely imperative that each member of our staff, as well as the student leaders with whom we work, be filled with the Holy Spirit if we are to have an effective ministry for Christ on the college campus.

There was a time in my own Christian ministry when I challenged Christians to witness and live holy lives for Christ, but the results were so discouraging that I began to devote most of my time and energies to evangelism, where God blessed with much more apparent results. However, as the years have passed, the Holy Spirit has helped me to see the great potential power in lukewarm Christians, if only they are awakened and harnessed for Christ. I am now convinced that the lukewarm, carnal Christian can be changed into a vital, dynamic, witnessing Christian, if he will surrender his will to Christ and be filled with the Holy Spirit. Again and again I am reminded of the great contrast between the church of Jesus Christ today and His Church of the first century.

What is the difference? What is that strange quality that sets one man apart from another when both are Christians? Some theologians would say that it is the degree of commitment, yet there are many people all over the world who are crying out to God, dedicating their lives to Christ day after day, and yet are continuing to be impotent and defeated. Why? Are we not told in Matthew 5:6, "Blessed are those who hunger and thirst for righteousness, for they shall be satisfied"?

Did not John, the beloved disciple, quote Jesus (1 John 1:5-7) as saying that God is light, and in Him is no darkness at all, and that if we walk in the "light" we have fellowship with the Father and the Son?

Christians need not live in spiritual poverty. The many thousands of promises recorded in the Word of God apply to every Christian. These promises include: assurance of God's love (John 3:16); eternal life (Romans 6:23); forgiveness of sin (1 John 1:9); provision of material needs (Philippians 4:19); the ordering of one's steps (Psalms 37:23); the secret of successful prayer (John 15:7); promise of an abundant life (John 10:10b); God's promise to honor a holy life (2 Chronicles 16:9); assurance that everything that happens is for our own good (Romans 8:28); deliverance from temptation (1 Corinthians 10:13); victory over fear (1 John 4:18); as well as thousands of others.

The Bible promises that every Christian can possess love, joy, peace, faith and many other beneficial qualities. What is wrong? Dr. Billy Graham has stated that at least 90% of all Christians in America are living defeated lives. Others who are in a position to know the spiritual pulse of America have made similar statements. It is quite likely that, according to the law of averages, you are among the 90%. You may have a heart for God. You read your Bible faithfully, you pray, you witness, you are active in your church; yet year after year you continue to fight a losing battle. Temptations come! Half-heartedly you resist, then yield, surrender and are finally defeated. For months you journey in the slough of despondency with Mr. Christian in Bunyan's *Pilgrim's Progress*. Then you attend a spiritual retreat and you are back on the Alpine heights for a brief time. Up, down, victories, defeats! Soon you cry out with Paul in Romans 7:24, "Wretched man that I am! Who will set me free from the body of this death?"

As president of Campus Crusade for Christ, it is my privilege to speak to thousands of students each year. At the conclusion of a message which I once gave at Princeton University, a devout young man approached me in great concern over his lack of "fruit" in witnessing. "I have tried to witness," he said, "but I have had no results. I read my Bible daily and pray and memorize Scripture. I attend every Christian meeting on campus. Yet, I have never been able to introduce another to Christ. What is wrong with me?" In counseling with him, I gently probed for the answer to his problem. I knew that he meant business. He wanted to please God, he sincerely wanted his friends to know his wonderful Savior, and, according to his conduct and Christian activities, he was a model Christian.

Jesus promises in John 14:26 and 16:13 that the Holy Spirit will teach us all things and will guide us into all truth. As I counseled with this young man, we were directed to some very important passages of Scripture. When he claimed these, by faith, they unlocked the door to victory and to unspeakable joy. He left the counseling room rejoicing and with an expectant heart. At that point, he began to experience a fruitful life in Christ such as he had never before known. He knew that something had happened in his life. He was a new man — no longer afraid, impotent and defeated. Now he was bold and had power and faith to believe God. He could hardly wait to see what God was going to do through him. "Lord," he prayed, "who will be the first to whom You will lead me today?"

In the course of the day, the Holy Spirit led this young Christian to a fellow student to whom he had previously witnessed without apparent success. But today was different. God had prepared the heart of the other student and soon these two were bowed in prayer as the student friend received Christ. The next day this marvelous experience was repeated with another student responding as if drawn by an invisible hand. This is not strange, for the Word of God tells us, "No one can come to Me, unless the Father... draws him" (John 6:44). Through the power of the Holy Spirit, this Princeton student continued to lead fellow students to Christ day after day. His own life was so wonderfully changed and empowered, so used of God, that he eventually became a Christian minister.

The story of the Princeton student is typical of hundreds of others who have sought counsel on campus after campus across the nation and around the world. There was a young minister who had earned his bachelor's and master's degrees in one of the finest theological seminaries of America, but was ineffective in his witnessing. Upon learning how he could appropriate the power of the Holy Spirit by faith, he experienced a new spirit of expectancy and joy that resulted in a victorious and fruitful life. There was a shy, timid student at a college retreat who expressed his concern for the lost, but was utterly frustrated and defeated by his fear of man. When God's power, victory, love and faith took possession of him, he experienced joy and fruit such as he had never believed possible. Fear and defeat gave way to courage, radiance and victory. Another faithful witness who heard, believed and received, discovered that witnessing was no longer a duty, but a joy! "It is just like being released from prison," he later exclaimed.

Countless additional examples such as those cited could be given of others whose fruitless and frustrated lives became fruitful and victorious when they received by faith the power of the Holy Spirit and discovered that the promises of Jesus were for them: "Follow Me and I will make you fishers of men" (Matthew 4:19); "By this is My Father glorified, that you bear much fruit" (John 15:8); "You did not choose Me, but I chose you, and appointed you, that you should go and bear fruit, and that your fruit should remain: that whatever you ask of the Father in My name, He may give to you" (John 15:16); "And without faith it is impossible to please Him, for he who comes to God must believe that He is, and that He is a rewarder of those who seek Him" (Hebrews 11:6).

Through the centuries there have been followers of Christ who were just ordinary Christians. Nothing spectacular ever happened to them or through them. Then, as happened to Peter and the disciples, something changed their lives. They were no longer ordinary or average. They became men and women of God, instruments of power. Their defeat turned to victory. Doubts and fear turned to assurance, joy and faith. They were the ones who "turned the world upside down" (Acts 17:6). Cowardly Peter, who denied Jesus three times (you and I have denied Him many more), became the bold Peter of Pentecost who preached fearlessly. On separate occasions, 3,000 and 5,000 believed in Christ and were added to the church. The early disciples possessed a stange new quality of life, a life of power which transformed the heart of a wicked Roman Empire during the first century. Their boldness led everyone of the twelve to a martyr's grave — except John, who died in exile on the Isle of Patmos.

The change in the lives of those to whom I have just referred all began at pentecost when those who were gathered together were filled with the Holy Spirit. Through this same power of the Holy Spirit, millions of others through the centuries have been changed into vital, dynamic Christians.

What do you know about the Holy Spirit? What does the Holy Spirit mean to you personally?

Jesus promised in His apostolic commission that the Holy Spirit would give us power to be His witnesses. "But you shall receive power when the Holy Spirit has come upon you; and you shall be My witnesses both in Jerusalem, and in all Judea and Samaria, and even to the remotest part of the earth" (Acts 1:8).

IT IS THE PURPOSE OF THIS BRIEF ARTICLE TO EXPLAIN HOW TO BE FILLED WITH THE HOLY SPIRIT AS IT RELATES TO THE FULFILLMENT OF THE GREAT COMMISSION OF OUR LORD. THERE- FORE, WE SHALL NOT DWELL ON THE MANY OTHER TRUTHS CONCERNING THE ROLE OF THE HOLY SPIRIT IN THE LIFE OF EVERY CHRISTIAN EXCEPT AS THEY CONTRIBUTE TO OUR MAJOR OBJECTIVE.

Let us now consider briefly come of these spiritual truths as they relate to the filling of the Holy Spirit.

I. WHO IS THE HOLY SPIRIT?

The Holy Spirit is the third person of the Trinity: Father, Son and *Holy Spirit.* He is not some vague, ethereal shadow nor an impersonal force. He is equal in every way with the Father and with the Son. All of the divine attributes are ascribed to the Holy Spirit. He has infinite intellect (1 Corinthians 2:11), will (1 Corinthians 12:11) and emotion (Romans 15:30).

Dr. J. Edwin Orr describes the Holy Spirit as "the Commander-in-Chief of the Army of Christ. He is the Lord of the harvest, supreme in revival, evangelism and missionary endeavor. Without His consent, plans are bound to fail. It behooves us as Christians to fit our tactical operations into the plan of His strategy, which is the reviving of the church and the evangelization of the world."

The first reference to the Holy Spirit is made in Genesis 1:2. His influence is noted throughout the Old Testament, but it becomes more pronounced in the life and ministry of our Lord. Finally, after our Savior ascended to be at the right hand of the Father, the place of power, He sent the Holy Spirit to be the "comforter" or "helper" (John 14:26 and 15:26). The Greek word for comforter or helper is *paraclete*, meaning the "one called along beside" the Christian as a companion and friend, also the one who "energizes," "strengthens" and "empowers" the believer in Christ.

The Holy Spirit is also called:

Spirit of God .... 1 Corinthians 3:16
Spirit of Christ .... Romans 8:9
Spirit of Life .... Romans 8:2
Spirit of Truth.................................. John 16:13
Spirit of Grace.............................. Hebrews 10:29
Spirit of Promise .... Ephesians 1:13

II. WHY DID THE HOLY SPIRIT COME?

The Holy Spirit came to bear witness to the Lord Jesus Christ and to glorify Him (John 16:13, 14). As Jesus had come to exalt and reveal the Father, the Holy Spirit was sent to exalt and glorify the Son, Jesus Christ.

It logically follows, then, that the more we allow the Holy Spirit to control our lives, the more we shall love and serve the Lord Jesus Christ, and the more we shall be conscious of His loving and abiding presence.

When we are filled with the Holy Spirit we are filled with Jesus Christ. Thus, when we are filled with the Holy Spirit — the Lord Jesus Christ — a power much greater than our own is released within us and through us for service and victorious living.

III. HOW IS THE HOLY SPIRIT RELATED TO EVERY CHRISTIAN?

(A Christian is one who has received Jesus Christ into his life as Lord and Savior, according to John 1:12; John 3:5; 2 Corinthians 5:17.)

At the time of spiritual birth:

A. The Holy Spirit regenerates men (John 3:5).

B. The Holy Spirit comes to dwell within each Christian (1 Corinthians 3:16).

C. The Holy Spirit seals every Christian in Christ (Ephesians 1:13; 4:30).

D. The Holy Spirit is the earnest or guarantee of the inheritance that each Christian will one day receive (2 Corinthians 5:5).

E. The Holy Spirit baptizes each Christian into the Body of Christ (1 Corinthians 12:13; Galatians 3:27; Romans 6:3, 4).

F. The Holy Spirit fills every yielded Christian for service.

At the moment of spiritual birth every Christian is regenerated, indwelt, sealed, guaranteed, baptized and filled with the Holy Spirit. The act of regenerating, indwelling, sealing, guaranteeing and baptizing the Christian into the Body of Christ by the Holy Spirit is a positional relationship and may or may not be accompanied by an emotional experience.

These truths do, however, acquaint the Christian with the thrilling fact of his union with Christ, ". . . you in Me, and I in you" (John 14:20). We exchange our weakness for His power, our sinfulness and defeat for His holiness and victory.

As a result of this relationship with Christ, every Christian has the potential to witness with power and to live a life of victory over sin. This potential power, the life of Jesus Christ in every believer, is released by faith as the Christian surrenders the control of his life to the Holy Spirit. Since it is the ministry of the Holy Spirit to glorify Christ, Jesus Christ now has unhindered opportunity to work in and through the believer to perform His perfect will.

Every Christian must be filled with the Holy Spirit in order to have the power to be a more effective witness for Christ. "But you shall receive power when the Holy Spirit has come upon you; and shall be My witnesses both in Jerusalem, and in all Judea and Samaria, and even to the remotest part of the earth" (Acts 1:8). Every biblical reference to the filling of the Holy Spirit, in both the Old Testament and in the New Testament, is related to power for service and witness.

The response to the filling of the Holy Spirit may vary from a calm assurance of power and quiet realization of a greater faith in Christ and the promises of His Word to a more emotional experience.

A careful study of 1 Corinthians 12 teaches us that all Christians are members of the Body of Christ. As various parts of the human body have different functions, so various members of Christ's body will have different responsibilities in His kingdom. No Christian should belittle another's gift. Neither should any Christian seek to imitate another in the "experience of filling" or in the gifts of the Holy Spirit. Every Christian must leave the assignment of the gifts, and the manner in which they are revealed, to the Holy Spirit.

Further, according to 1 Corinthians 13, any or all of these gifts will profit little unless we are motivated by love.

We are admonished by God in Ephesians 5:17-20, "So then do not be foolish, but understand what the will of the Lord is. And do not get drunk with wine, for that is dissipation, but be filled with the Spirit, speaking to one another in psalms and hymns and spiritual songs, singing and making melody with your heart to the Lord; always giving thanks for all things in the name of our Lord Jesus Christ to God, even the Father."

The apostle Paul was suggesting that a Spirit-filled Christian will know God's will, and may give the impression of being "Spirit-intoxicated" because of the joy, radiance, boldness and courage that he frequently demonstrates. Also, as this Scripture passage suggests, a Spirit-filled Christian is continually praising God in his heart and giving thanks for all things. He realizes, in a way that he could not while in his carnal state, that all that he is and has is by the grace of God.

Beginning with the day of Pentecost and continuing through the centuries, the work of God has always been accomplished through men who were filled with the Holy Spirit — men such as Peter, Paul and all of the disciples.

In more recent times there have been men like John Wesley, Jonathan Edwards, Charles Finney, Dwight L. Moody, Charles Spurgeon, G. Campbell Morgan, R. A. Torrey and scores of other Christian leaders — some of whom are now living — who have been filled with the Holy Spirit and who have been greatly used to further the cause of Christ and His kingdom. However, the filling of the Holy Spirit is not limited to Christian leaders, but is available to all Christians who meet God's terms.

Hear what some of these men and women of God say about the importance of every Christian's being filled with the Holy Spirit:

"... Men ought to seek with their whole hearts to be filled with the

Spirit of God. Without being filled with the Spirit, it is utterly impossible that an individual Christian or a church can ever live or work as God desires . . ."

— Andrew Murray

"Christians are as guilty for not being filled with the Holy Spirit as sinners are for not repenting. They are even more so, for as they have more light, they are so much the more guilty."

— Charles G. Finney

"The Spirit-filled life, that life that permits His fullness in a sustained overflow, is the only life that can please God."

— Norman B. Harrison

"The great purpose in the filling of the Holy Spirit is power for service. The best and most-used Christians known to me have been men who have testified to a deeper experience of the filling of the Holy Spirit."

— J. Edwin Orr

"I believe that it is impossible for any Christian to be effective either in his life or in his service unless he is filled with the Holy Spirit who is God's only provision of power."

— Henrietta C. Mears

"Read the biographies of God's men and you will discover that each one sought and obtained the induement of power from on high. One sermon preached in the anointing is worth a thousand in the energy of the flesh."

— Dr. Oswald J. Smith

I wish again to make it especially clear at this point that the Holy Spirit already indwells every believer and the special enduement of power that attends the filling of the Holy Spirit is not reserved for Christian leaders only. Every Christian not only has the prerogative of being filled with the Holy Spirit, but every Christian is admonished to be filled with the Spirit (Ephesians 5:18). Therefore, if a Christian is not filled, he is disobedient to the command of God and is sinning against God. Further, since God commands us in His Word to be filled with the Spirit, we may be certain that he has the power to fill us the very moment we invite Him to do so.

I assure you that, according to the promises of the Word of God and from observations and personal experience, Jesus is far more eager to give His love and forgiveness, His power for service, and a life of victory over sin than we are to receive them. Jesus is far more eager to fill us with the Holy Spirit than you and I are to be filled.

Why, then, are so many Christians living in defeat? Why are so few Christians effective witnesses for Christ? Why are so few Christians living lives that are filled with the Holy Spirit? These questions bring us to the next important step in preparation for being filled with the Spirit.

IV. WHAT IS THE SPIRIT-FILLED LIFE?

The Spirit-filled life is the Christ-filled life. The Spirit-filled Christian is one who, according to Romans 6:11, has considered himself to be dead to sin, but alive to God in Christ Jesus. Christ is now on the throne of the life. He is Lord! The Holy Spirit came to exalt and glorify Jesus Christ. In order to be filled with the Holy Spirit a Christian must be dead to self. When he is dead to self, the Lord Jesus Christ, who now has unhindered control of his life, can begin to express His love through him. The One to whom "all power in heaven and in earth is given," and "in whom dwells all the fullness of the Godhead bodily," can now express that power through the Spirit-filled Christian. The One who came to seek and to save the lost, now begins to seek the lost through the Christian. He directs the Christian's steps to those who are lost and to those who are in need. He begins to use the Christian's lips to tell of His love. His great heart of compassion becomes evident in the Spirit-filled life.

Actually, in a very real sense, the Christian gives up *his* life, *his* impotence and defeat for the power and victory of Jesus Christ. This is what the great missionary statesman Hudson Taylor referred to as the "exchanged life." When a Christian is filled with the Holy Spirit, he is filled with Jesus Christ. He no longer thinks of Christ as One who helps to do some kind of Christian task but, rather, Jesus Christ does the work through the Christian. He does not want us to work for Him. He wants us to let Him do His work through us. This is that glorious experience that the apostle Paul knew when he said in Galatians 2:20, "I have been crucified with Christ; and it is no longer I who live, but Christ lives in me." The Christian's body now becomes Christ's body to use as He wills; the mind becomes His mind to think His thoughts; the will is now controlled by His will; the total personality, time and talents are now completely His.

The beloved apostle goes on to say, ". . . and the life which I now live in the flesh I live by faith in the Son of God, who loved me, and delivered Himself up for me." Whose faith? The faith of the Son of God, the One who loved us and gave Himself for us, the One to whom "all power in heaven and earth is given." Think of it! Can you grasp what this means? If you can, and if you yield your will to God the Holy Spirit and acknowledge that Jesus Christ is in your life moment by moment, you are in for a great adventure. The Lord Jesus Christ will begin to draw scores of lost men and women to Himself through your yielded, Spirit-filled life.

V. WHY ARE SO FEW CHRISTIANS FILLED WITH THE HOLY SPIRIT?

Basically, the problem involves the will. Man is a free moral agent. He was created by God with a mind and will of his own.

God would be breaking His own spiritual laws if He *forced* man to do His bidding. At the time of conversion the will of man is temporarily yielded to the will of God. In Romans 10:9, Paul tells us that, if we confess with our mouths Jesus as Lord, and believe in our hearts that God has raised Him from the dead, we shall be saved. Man must be willing to "repent," which means to turn from his own way to go God's way, before he can become a child of God. However, after conversion, the heart frequently loses its "first love." The radiance and glow that accompanied the spiritual birth experience are gone, and many Christians no longer walk in "the light as He Himself is in the light" (1 John 1:7). They no longer seek to do the will of God, but for various reasons, have chosen to go their own way. They have chosen to work out their own plan and purpose for life. Believing themselves to be free, they become servants of sin and finally they say with the apostle Paul in Romans 7:19, 20, 24: "For the good that I wish, I do not do; but I practice the very evil that I do not wish. But if I am doing the very thing I do not wish, I am no longer the one doing it, but sin which dwells in me. Wretched man that I am! Who will set me free from the body of this death?" There is no one more miserable than a Christian out of fellowship with Christ.

In this spiritual condition there is no longer any joy in the Christian walk, no longer any desire to witness for Christ, no concern for those who are desperately in need of the forgiveness and love of our Savior.

What are the reasons, then, that one who has experienced the love and forgiveness that only Christ can give, one who has experienced the joy of His presence, would reject the will of God and choose to go his own way? Why would a Christian sacrifice the power and dynamic of the Spirit-filled life in order to have his own way?

There are several reasons:

A. *Lack of knowledge of the Word of God:* God's Word contains glorious truths concerning the relationship that the Christian has with the Lord Jesus Christ, God the Father and the Holy Spirit. This lack of information has kept many from appropriating the fullness of the Holy Spirit. Think of it — every Christian is a Child of God (John 1:12). His sins have been forgiven and he may continue to be cleansed from all sin (1 John 1:7) as he continues in fellowship with Christ. God the Father, Son and Holy Spirit actually dwell in the heart of every Christian, waiting to empower and bring each child of God to his full maturity in Christ. (Review again Part III. How is the Holy Spirit related to every Christian?)

B. *Pride:* Pride has kept many Christians from being filled with the Holy Spirit. Pride was the sin of Satan (Isaiah 14:12-14). Pride was the first sin of man as Adam and Eve wanted to be something they were not. Pride is at the root of most of man's self-imposed estrangement from God. The self-centered, egocentric Christian cannot have fellowship with God: ". . . for God is opposed to the proud, but gives grace to the humble" (1 Peter 5:5).

C. *Fear:* Fear of man keeps many Christians from being filled with the Holy Spirit. "The fear of man brings a snare" (Proverbs 29;25). One of the greatest tragedies of our day is the general practice among Christians of conforming to the conduct and standards of a non-Christian society. Many are afraid to be different; ashamed to witness for the One "who loved us and gave Himself for us." Remember, in 1 Peter 2:9 we are told: "But you are a chosen race, a royal priesthood, a holy nation, a people for God's own possession, that you may proclaim the excellencies of Him who has called you out of darkness into His marvelous light." The Lord favors those who fear (reverence which leads to obedience) Him" (Psalm 147:11). Jesus said, "For whoever is ashamed of Me and My words, of him shall the Son of Man be ashamed" (Luke 9:26).

Many Christians are fearful of being thought fanatical by their fellow Christians and others should they be filled with the Holy Spirit.

D. *Secret sin:* Unconfessed sin keeps many Christians from being filled with the Holy Spirit. Perhaps God has reminded you of a lie you have told that has damaged someone's reputation; or stolen merchandise or money that has not been returned; or an unethical transaction; or cheating on an exam, or any number of acts that He wants you to confess to Him. He may lead you to make restitution to those whom you have wronged (Matthew 5:23, 24). If so, be obedient to His leading. We may be able to hide these things from our friends and others, but we cannot hide them from God. "Would not God find this out? For He knows the secrets of the heart" (Psalm 44:21). Is there anyone whom you have not forgiven? If, so, God will not forgive you (Mark 11:24-26). However, if we confess these sins to God as the Lord directs us, we are forgiven and cleansed (1 John 1:9).

E. *Worldly-mindedness:* A love for material things and a desire to conform to the ways of a secular society keep many Christians from being filled with the Holy Spirit. "Do not love the world, nor the things in the world. If anyone loves the world, the love of the Father is not in him. For all that is in the world, the lust of the flesh, and the lust of the eyes and the boastful pride of life, is not from the Father, but is from the world. And the world is passing away, and also its lusts; but the one who does the will of God abides forever" (1 John 2:15-17). Man lives a brief span of years and is gone from the earthly scene. Every Christian should make careful and frequent evaluation of how he invests his time, talents and treasure in order to accomplish the most for the cause of Christ. "Only one life, will soon be past; only what's done for Christ will last."

"No one can serve two masters; for either he will hate the one and love the other, or he will hold to one and despise the other. You cannot serve God and Mammon. But seek first His kingdom, and His righteousness; and all these things shall be added to you" (Matthew 6:24, 33).

F. *Lack of trust in God:* This keeps many Christians from making a full surrender of their wills to Him and from being filled with the Holy Spirit. Many Christians have a fear that amounts almost to super-stition that, if they surrender themselves fully to God, something tragic will happen to test them. They may fear that they will lose a loved one. Some fear that God will send them to some remote section of the world as a missionary to some savage tribe, against their wills.

I remember well a young lad who had such fears — he was afraid that God would change his plans. As we reasoned together, I reminded him that God's love was so great that He sent His only begotten Son to die for his sins. We spoke of a Savior who loved him so much that He gladly gave His life on the cross and shed His blood for his sins. Then I asked the question, "Can you trust a God like that?" He replied, "I had never thought of it that way — I can and will trust Him." Today this young man has finished seminary and is a member of our Campus

Crusade staff. He is one of the most fruitful and victorious Christians I know.

You can trust God with your life, your loved ones, your money, your future, everything! Not only is He a loving Father, but God's love is wiser than that of any earthly father and is more tender than that of any earthly mother. So do not be afraid to trust God with your whole life, every moment of every day, and He will fill you with His Holy Spirit.

I have two sons whom I love dearly. Suppose, when they were very young, they had come to me and said, "Daddy, we love you and have been thinking about how we can show our love for you. We have decided that we will do anything that you want us to do." Now, how would I have responded? Would I have said, "Boys, I have been waiting for just this moment. Now that you have relinquished your wills to mine, I am going to lock you in your rooms, give away all your favorite possessions, and make you do all of the things that you most dislike to do. You will regret the day you were born. I will make you the most miserable boys on this block."

How ridiculous! I would have responded by trying to demonstrate my love for them in an even greater way. In the same way, our heavenly Father is ready to bless and enrich our lives the moment we yield our wills, our all, to Him.

These and many other experiences of defeat have kept Christians from experiencing the joy of the Spirit-filled life. For example, do any of the following apply to you?

An exalted feeling of your own importance
Love of human praise
Anger and impatience
Self-will, stubbornness, unteachability
A compromising spirit
Jealous disposition
Lustful, unholy actions
Dishonesty
Unbelief
Selfishness
Love of money, beautiful clothes, cars, houses and land

Some of you may wonder, "Is it necessary for me to gain victory over all of my defeats and frustrations before I can be filled with the Holy Spirit?" Absolutely not! Just as Jesus Christ is the only one who can forgive your sins, so the Holy Spirit is the only one who can give victory and power.

VI. HOW CAN A CHRISTIAN BE FILLED WITH THE HOLY SPIRIT?

First, we need to know that just as people have many different experiences when they receive Jesus Christ as Lord and Savior, so they have different experiences when they are filled with the Holy Spirit. For example, one man responds to the invitation to receive Christ in an evangelistic campaign, another kneels quietly in the privacy of his home and receives Christ. Both are born again, and their lives are changed by the power of Christ. Of course, there are scores of other circumstances and experiences through which sincere men meet the Savior and become "new creatures in Christ."

In like manner, and in different ways, sincere Christians are filled with the Spirit. It should be made clear at this point that to be "filled with the Spirit" does not mean that we receive more of the Holy Spirit, but that we give Him more of ourselves. As we yield our lives to the Holy Spirit and are filled with His presence, He has greater freedom to work in and through our lives, to control us in order to better exalt and glorify Christ.

God is too great to be placed in a man-made mold. However, there are certain spiritual laws that are inviolate. Since the Holy Spirit already dwells within every Christian, it is no longer necessary to "wait in Jerusalem" as Jesus instructed the disciples to do, except to make personal preparation for His empowering. The Holy Spirit will fill us with His power the moment we are fully yielded. It is possible for a man to be at a quiet retreat and become filled with the Holy Spirit. It is likewise possible for a man to be filled with the Holy Spirit while walking down a busy street in a great city. Such was the experience of Dwight L. Moody. It is even possible for a man to be filled with the Holy Spirit and know something wonderful has happened, yet be completely ignorant at the time of what has actually taken place, provided he has a genuine desire to yield his will to the Lord Jesus Christ.

I do not want to suggest that the steps which I am about to propose are the only way in which one can be filled with the Holy Spirit. This spiritual formula is offered, first, because it is scriptural, and second, because I know from experience that it works.

Do you want to be filled with the Holy Spirit? What are your motives? Are you looking for some ecstatic experience, or do you sincerely desire to serve the Lord Jesus Christ with greater power and effectiveness? Do you want, with all of your heart, to help others find Christ?

This is the spiritual formula that I urge you to prayerfully consider:

A. *We are commanded to be filled with the Spirit.*

"And do not get drunk with wine, for that is dissipation, but be filled with the Spirit" (Ephesians 5:18). This is an admonition of God. Do you think that He would ask you to do something beyond that which you are able to experience?

B. *We shall receive power for witnessing when we are filled.*

"But you shall receive power when the Holy Spirit has come upon you; and you shall be My witnesses both in Jerusalem, and in all Judea and Samaria, and even to the remotest part of the earth" (Acts 1:8). If you have no desire to be Jesus Christ's witness or if you have no power in your witness, you may be sure that you are not filled with the Holy Spirit. The Holy Spirit came in order for the disciples — and for you and me — to receive power. Why do we need power? To be Christ's witnesses right where we are and in the remotest part of the earth. Can you sincerely say that this is your motive for wanting to be filled with the Spirit?

C. *If any man is thirsty, let him come to Me and drink.*

"Now on the last day, the great day of the feast, Jesus stood and cried out, saying, 'If any man is thirsty, let him come to Me and drink. He who believes in Me, as the Scripture said, "From his innermost being shall flow rivers of living water." ' But this He spoke of the Spirit, whom those who believed in Him were to receive; for the Spirit was not yet given, because Jesus was not yet glorified" (John 7:37-39). "Blessed are those who hunger and thirst for righteousness, for they shall be satisfied" (Matthew 5:6).

When a Christian is ready to respond to the gracious invitation of our blessed Savior, "If any man is thirsty, let him come to Me and drink," he is ready to relinquish his will for the will of God. Therefore, this third step involves a complete surrender of your will, without reservation, to the will of God. You have come to the place where you joyfully anticipate knowing and doing His will because you know God is loving and trustworthy and that His will is best.

Up until this moment the Holy Spirit has been just a "guest" in your life, for He came to live in you the moment you became a Christian. Sometimes He was locked up in a small closet, while you used the rest of the house for your own pleasure.

Now you want him to be more than a guest — as a matter of fact, you want to turn over the title deed of your life to Him and give Him the keys to every room. You invite the Holy Spirit into the library of your mind, the dining room of your appetites, the parlor of your relationships, the game room of your social life. You invite Him into the small hidden rooms where you have previously engaged in secret, shameful activities. All of this is past. Now, He is the Master! The challenge of Romans 12:1, 2 has become clear and meaningful to you and you want to ". . . present your body a living and holy sacrifice, acceptable to God, which is your spiritual service of worship." And you no longer want to be conformed to this world, but you want to be transformed by the renewing of your mind, "that you may prove what the will of God is, that which is good and acceptable and perfect."

Now you know that your body is the temple of the Holy Spirit who lives within you. You are not your own anymore for you were bought with the precious blood of the Lord Jesus; therefore, you now want to glorify God in your body and in your spirit, which are God's (1 Corinthians 6:19, 20).

Now, with all of your heart, you want to seek first the kingdom of God (Matthew 6:33).

Now you want to seek "the things above, where Christ is, seated at the right hand of God. For you have died, and your life is hidden with Christ in God" (Colossians 3:1, 3).

Now you can say with joy unspeakable, as Paul did, "I have been crucified with Christ; and it is no longer I who live, but Christ lives in me; and the life which I now live in the flesh I live by faith in the Son of God, who loved me, and delivered Himself up for me" (Galatians 2:20). You have exchanged your life for the life of Christ.

If you can say these things and mean them with all of your heart, you are ready for the fourth step. However, before we take up the discussion of this next step, I feel constrained to call your attention to the words of our Savior found in John 15:18, 20. "If the world hates you, you know that it has hated Me before it hated you . . .' A slave is not great than his master.' If they persecuted Me, they will also persecute you."

The Spirit-filled Christian life is not any easy one, though it is a life filled with adventure and thrills, the likes of which one cannot possibly experience in any other way. Whether or not we are Christians, we are going to have problems in this life. Christians or not, we will one day die. If I am going to be a Christian, I want all that God has for me and I want to be all that he wants me to be. If I am to suffer at all, and one day die, why not suffer and die for the highest and best, for the Lord Jesus Christ and His gospel!

Before we leave this thought, let me ask you a question. Have you ever heard of one of God's saints who has suffered for the cause of Christ express any regrets? I never have! I have heard only praise, adoration and thanksgiving to God for the privilege of serving Christ, no matter how difficult the task. On the other hand, I have heard many who have received Christ late in life tell how sorry they are that they waited so long. Do not develop a martyr's complex, but do not expect a "bed of roses" either.

Now for the next step in receiving the fullness of the Holy Spirit.

D. *We appropriate the filling of the Holy Spirit by faith.*

Remember that, if you are a Christian, God the Father, Son and Holy Spirit are already living within you. Great spiritual power and resources are available to you. Like a miser starving to death with a fortune in boxes and jars about his cluttered room, many Christians are starving spiritually, living in defeat, failing to utilize the spiritual fortune that is their heritage in Christ.

In Ephesians 5:18, Paul admonishes, "And do not get drunk with wine, for that is dissipation, but be filled with the Spirit."

Further, in 1 John 5:14, 15, we are assured, "And this is the confidence which we have before Him, that, if we ask anything according to His will, He hears us. And if we know that he hears us in whatever we ask, we know that we have the requests that we have asked from Him." We know that it is God's will that we be filled with His Spirit. Therefore, as we ask the Holy Spirit to fill us, we can know according to the Word of God that our prayer is answered.

Like our salvation, the filling of the Holy Spirit is a gift of God — we do not and cannot earn either. Both are received by the complete yielding of our wills, in faith, when we have confessed our sins and met the other conditions mentioned in Lesson Four.

Here is a review of the steps that we have discussed in preparation for the filling of the Holy Spirit:

1. We are admonished to be filled.

2. We are promised power for service when we are filled.

3. We are to yield our will to God's will and seek first the kingdom of God.

4. We are to appropriate the filling of the Holy Spirit by faith.

E. *We must expect to be filled.*

"And without faith it is impossible to please Him, for he who comes to God must believe that he is, and that he is a rewarder of those who seek Him" (Hebrews 11:6).

Do you believe God wants you to be filled with the Holy Spirit?

Do you believe God has the power to fill you with the Holy Spirit?

In Matthew 9:28, 29, Jesus talked to the blind men and asked of them, "Do you believe that I am able to do this?" They said to Him, "Yes, Lord." Then He touched their eyes, saying, "Be it done to you according to your faith."

Find a quiet place where you can be alone and read again the portions of Scripture given in the preceding paragraphs. You do not have to wait for the Holy Spirit. He is already dwelling within you if you are a Christian. He is waiting for you to allow Him to fill you. Remember, "Be it done to you according to your faith." "He is a rewarder of those who seek Him."

Have you honestly yielded your life to Christ, your will to His will?

Do you believe that you are filled with the Holy Spirit at this moment? If so, thank Him that you are filled. Thank Him for His indwelling presence and power. Thank Him by faith for victory over defeat and for effectiveness in witnessing. Praise God and give thanks continually (Ephesians 5:20; 1 Thessalonians 5:18).

VII. HOW CAN A CHRISTIAN KNOW WHEN HE IS FILLED WITH THE HOLY SPIRIT?

There are two very good ways of knowing when you are filled with the Holy Spirit.

First, by the promises of the Word of God. And second, by personal experience.

If you have faithfully yielded to the will of God and sincerely surrendered your way to Him in accordance with the steps outlined in this presentation, if you have asked Him to fill you — He has done it! "And this is the confidence which we have before Him, that, if we ask anything according to His will, He hears us. And if we know that he hears us in whatever we ask, we know that we have the requests that we have asked from Him" (1 John 5:14, 15). Is it His will that you be filled, according to Ephesians 5:18? Then, can you believe that He has heard you? Now, can you know that you have the petitions that you desired of Him?

God's Word promises us that we can know. Therefore, on the basis of His Word you can know that you are filled, if you have met the conditions which are given in His Word.

What about feelings? You may or may not have an emotional response at the time you kneel in prayer and ask for the filling of the

Spirit. In counseling with many students, as well as adults, I have found that the majority experience a calm assurance that they are filled, and with this assurance comes a spirit of expectancy that God is going to use them in a way they have never been used before to introduce others to Christ. Greater faith in God and His Word is born in the hearts of those who have been filled with the Holy Spirit. Results? Greater faith, power, boldness and effectiveness in witnessing.

First, there is the fact of God's promise in His Word. Then there is the exercise of faith in the trustworthiness of God and His promises. Faith in the fact is followed by feeling. Remember: fact, faith and feelings — in that order.

VIII. WHAT RESULTS CAN ONE EXPECT FROM BEING FILLED WITH THE HOLY SPIRIT?

Now comes the real test that will determine if you are truly filled with the Holy Spirit. As time goes on, do you find that you have a greater love for Christ? Are you more concerned for those who do not know His love and forgiveness? Are you experiencing a greater faith, boldness, liberty and power in witnessing? If so, you are filled with the Spirit. Jesus Christ is beginning to express His life and love through and in you.

Remember, Jesus promised that we would receive power after the Holy Spirit has come upon us. After receiving power we will naturally want to be His witnesses wherever we are (Acts 1:8).

It is definitely true that you will have a greater love for Christ, for your fellowman and for the Word of God when you are filled with the Holy Spirit. Also, the fruit of the Spirit, as described in Galatians 5:22, 23, will become more evident in your life.

However, we must remember that there is a difference between the fruit of the Spirit and the gifts of the Spirit.

The filling of the Holy Spirit is given for power and boldness in witnessing for Christ. Many Christian leaders agree with Dr. R. A. Torrey, who said, "I have gone through my Bible time and time again checking this subject and I make this statement without the slightest fear of successful contradiction that there is not one single passage in the Old Testament or the New Testament where the filling with the Holy Spirit is spoken of, where it is not connected with testimony for service."

We hasten to add that as a Christian abides in Christ, living in the fullness of the Spirit, the fruit of the Spirit — love, joy, peace, patience, kindness, goodness, faithfulness, gentleness and self-control, listed in Galatians 5:22, 23 — is developed and the Christian becomes more mature spiritually. The maturing of the fruit of the Spirit is a lifetime process which goes on continually as Christ is being formed in the life of the Christian. Some Christians give greater evidence of the fruit of the Spirit than do others, because of a greater degree of yieldedness to His working. The more we acknowledge ourselves to be dead to sin and give allegiance to the Lord Jesus Christ and His life within us, and the more we allow Him through the power of the Holy Spirit to live out His life through us, the more evident will be the fruit of the Spirit.

The development and maturing of the fruit of the Spirit is a long process, but the gifts of the Holy Spirit are given at the time a person becomes a Christian. Though every Christian who is filled with the

Spirit receives power for witnessing, not every Christian receives the same gift, according to 1 Corinthians 12. Some are called to be apostles, some prophets, other evangelists, pastors and teachers (Ephesians 4:11). Therefore, we must let the Lord direct us into His place of service for us.

Do not try to imitate the ministry of someone else. Be patient. Do not try to decide what you should do with your life or where you should serve Christ. He will express His life in and through you as you continue to study His Word and remain obedient and sensitive to the leading of the Holy Spirit. Through God's Word and the leading of the Holy Spirit, you will discover what God's will is for you.

IX. IS THERE MORE THAN ONE FILLING OF THE HOLY SPIRIT?

Yes, there are many fillings of the Spirit for the yielded Christian. We should be filled for each new opportunity of Christian service. The admonition to be filled with the Holy Spirit in Ephesians 5:18 literally means, in the original Greek, to be filled with the Spirit constantly and continually — to keep on being filled. The Scriptures record several instances where Peter and the disciples were filled with the Spirit.

X. HOW CAN A CHRISTIAN CONTINUE TO BE FILLED WITH THE HOLY SPIRIT?

The Christian is utterly and wholly dependent upon the Holy Spirit for all spiritual victory and power. Therefore, the more yielded he is, the more liberty the Holy Spirit will have in working through his life in bringing others to Christ and bringing him to spiritual maturity in Christ.

Here are some practical suggestions that will assist you to live in the fullness of the Spirit:

A. Meditate on these glorious truths: Jesus Christ literally dwells within you. You are dead to self and sin and to all personal and selfish desires. You are alive to God through Jesus Christ (Romans 6:11). Remember, you have exchanged your life with all of its sin, frustrations and defeats for the victorious and triumphant life of Christ, in whom "all the fullness of deity dwells in bodily form, and in Him you have been made complete" (Colossians 2:9, 10). Just think, the one who dwells in your heart is the one who claims all power in heaven and in earth! This is why the apostle Paul said, "I can do all things through Him who strengthens me" (Philippians 4:13). You have buried "Old Adam," screwed the lid down on the coffin and covered him over with six feet of sod. Jesus Christ is not helping you to live the Christian life with your old sin nature. Rather He is now using your body as His Temple, your mind to think His thoughts, your heart to express His love and compassion, your lips to speak His truths.

His will has become your will. At first you may find it necessary to acknowledge and confirm many, many times during the day that this transaction has taken place. You may find it necessary to change your whole way of thinking and praying. Don't think, "What can I do for Christ?" or pray, "God, use me to do this or that for You." Pray rather, "Lord Jesus, I am Yours totally and completely without reservation. Use me as You wish. Send me wherever You will, for I am dead and my life is hid with Christ in God." Seek to abide in Christ (1 John 2:6). What is involved in abiding in Christ? Jesus said, "If you keep My commandments, you will abide in My love..." (John 15:10a).

To abide is to keep His commandments. To keep His commandments is to obey. The abiding life is an effortless life. How slowly do we arrive at this simple fact, that true New Testament living is effortless.

A branch does not try to produce fruit, any more than the electric light bulb tries to shine. Neither has any need to try; they simply draw upon an inexhaustible supply of life and energy. In doing so they scarcely touch the fringe of their resources. The Christian has infinitely greater resources. The one who created vegetable life and electric energy is the one who lives in us. Why do we need to try? Only because we are not abiding. The truest test of Christian living is, am I trying or am I abiding? If I find myself still trying, I am not as yet an unchoked channel through which His life may flow.

Meditate on the following portions of Scripture: John 14, 15 and 16; Matthew 6; Colossians 3; Ephesians 5; Romans 6, 8, 12 and 14; 1 Corinthians 13; 1 John 1; Hebrews 11; Galatians 5; and Psalm 37:1-7, 23, 24.

I suggest that you secure a notebook and make an outline of each of these chapters, listing especially those suggestions that you feel will aid you in abiding in Christ. Continue to use your notebook for outlining other portions of Scripture and for recording key verses you would like to memorize. There are many other portions of Scripture that will help you to abide in Christ.

B. Make it a practice to spend definite time each day in prayer for God's guidance of your life and for the souls of men. Make a list of people whom you would like to have find Christ. Pray for them daily (Ephesians 6:18 and 1 Samuel 12:23).

C. Spend time daily reading and studying the Word of God. Make a practice of memorizing key portions of Scripture (see Hebrews 4:12; 1 Corinthians 2:9-12; Psalm 119:4, 9, 15, 16, 97, 98, 103, 105, 130).

D. Do not grieve the Holy Spirit. Confess and turn from sinful practices. 1 John 1:9 says, "If we confess our sins, He is faithful and righteous to forgive us our sins and to cleanse us from all unrighteousness." The moment you do something you know is wrong, you will grieve the Holy Spirit if you do not confess it. What do we mean by grieving the Holy Spirit? The Spirit is holy and He is displeased and saddened when a Christian commits sin and continues its practice. Therefore, if you want to continue to be filled with the Holy Spirit and to have power in witnessing for Christ, live a yielded, holy life.

E. Do not quench the Holy Spirit. Be sensitive to the leading of the Holy spirit for He is omniscient. He has infinite wisdom and knowledge and will lead us into all truth (John 16:13). Never say "no" to Him. As you grow accustomed to the Spirit-filled, Christ-directed life, you will have many wonderful experiences such as Philip had (Acts 8:26-29) when the Holy Spirit led him to speak to the Ethiopian; and as Paul had (Acts 16:9) when he was called to Macedonia to preach the gospel.

The most thrilling experiences of my entire life have been those when the still, small voice of the Spirit spoke to my heart, telling me to speak to people about Christ, and, as I have talked with them in obedience to the Spirit's leading, I have always discovered that the Holy Spirit had prepared their hearts for my witness. Many times I have been told, "Bill, the Lord sent you to me." Or "Everything you have said has been for me. Someone must have told you of my problem." The Spirit knows all things, and if you and I are filled with His presence and power, we will always have the right thing to say to those who are in need.

There have been many such thrilling leadings of the Spirit, but I shall share only one.

One day my wife, Vonette, and I were driving to the Forest Home Christian Conference Center for a session of the College Briefing Conference that has been so greatly used of God in the lives of thousands of collegians. It was an extremely hot day late in August and our car developed a vapor lock and refused to run as we started up the mountian. We waited for the motor to cool and finally, after a considerable delay, we got the car started.

We drove into the yard of a nearby rural home to ask for water to fill the radiator. The man of the house was very generous and gracious. He helped me fill the radiator with water, but even though we were there five or ten minutes, I did not speak to him about Christ. My mind was on an important meeting up the mountain that we wanted badly to attend. As I leaned over to pick up the radiator cap, which had blown off, my New Testament fell out of my shirt pocket. Still I did not hear that still, small voice of the Spirit. We had thanked the man for his kindness and were driving out of his yard when suddenly I felt a strong compulsion to return to talk with this man about Christ. "But," I argued as we discussed it, "we are late for the meeting now. Anyway, he would think we are crackpots if we were to go back. Besides, if I were going to witness to him about Christ, I should have done it when he was helping me fill the radiator with water."

Human arguments are futile against the insistent voice of the Spirit, and after we had driven a couple of miles, we turned around and headed back. As an added precaution we pulled over to the side of the road for prayer. "Lord, don't let us make a mistake — this seems so foolish. Give us the words to say. May Your will be done."

As we drove into the yard, the man came out on the porch to greet us. "Did you forget something?" he asked. "Yes, we did forget something, sir. I know this may sound a little strange, but we are Christians and we felt that the Lord wanted us to come back to talk to you about Christ." There was no need to say more for, as I spoke, tears began to gather and trickle down his cheeks. His chin began to tremble as he told us that he knew the Lord had sent us. He asked us to come inside and as we went in, he called his wife.

He said, "I used to go to church years ago, but I fell into sin and I haven't been back in many years. This week my wife has been attending a revival meeting here in town and more and more, with each passing day, I have been burdened with the weight of my sins. I want to get right with God." We all knelt there in his living room and both he and his wife committed their lives and their home to Christ. We went on our way, praising God for the leading of His Holy Spirit and for another opportunity to witness for our blessed Savior.

As you ask God to fill you with the Holy Spirit, you are about to begin the greatest adventure of your life. Remember that you are asking to be filled with the Holy Spirit rather than filled with self. As He takes control of your life, you will become more like Christ. The Holy Spirit is not the author of confusion and emotional extremes. He has come to exalt and glorify Jesus; therefore, when you are filled with the Holy Spirit, it will be your constant desire to do the will of God and that which will please and honor Jesus Christ.

Why did Jesus come into this world? "To seek and to save that which was lost" (Luke 19:10).

What will please Him most? We shall please Him most as we help fulfill His Great Commission, by going into all the world and preaching the gospel to every creature and letting Him live His life through us.

How is this to be accomplished? By the power of the Holy Spirit.

Think of it — you and I are privileged to be used by our Savior in helping to reach a lost world with the glorious "good news"!

We dare not sin against the Lord and against those who are waiting to hear by hesitating another moment.

Ask Him to fill you now!

Bill Bright
Founder and President
Campus Crusade for Christ International
Arrowhead Springs, San Bernardino, California

LESSON ONE

WHO IS THE HOLY SPIRIT AND WHY DID HE COME?

BE SURE YOU HAVE READ THE ARTICLE ABOUT THE HOLY SPIRIT BEFORE YOU START THIS LESSON.

Introduction

OBJECTIVE: To become acquainted with the Holy Spirit and to understand His mission.

TO MEMORIZE: John 16:13, 14.

TO READ: John 3:1-8; Romans 8.

HOLY SPIRIT

Bible Study

A. *Who the Holy Spirit is*

The Holy Spirit is a person, the third person of the Trinity: Father, Son and Holy Spirit. He is not some vague, ethereal shadow, nor an impersonal force. He is a person equal in every way with the Father and the Son. All of the divine attributes ascribed to the Father and the Son are equally ascribed to the Holy Spirit.

1. Personality (a person) is composed of intellect, emotions and will. In 1 Corinthians 2:11, what indicates that the Holy Spirit has intellect? _____

   What evidence is there in Romans 15:30 that the Holy Spirit has emotion? _____

   How do you see the Holy Spirit exercising His will in 1 Corinthians 12:11? _____

2. What do you understand about the nature of the Holy Spirit from the following references?

   Romans 8:2 _____

   John 16:13 _____

   Hebrews 10:29 _____

   Romans 1:4 _____

3. What about His function or His role?

John 14:26 _____

1 Corinthians 3:16 _____

John 16:13, 14 _____

B. *Why He came*

1. What is the chief reason the Holy Spirit came (John 16:14)? _____

2. What will be a logical result when the Holy Spirit controls your life? _____

LOVE
JOY
PEACE
PATIENCE
KINDNESS
FAITHFULNESS
GOODNESS

CHRIST CENTERED
EMPOWERED BY H.S.
INTRODUCES OTHERS TO CHRIST
EFFECTIVE PRAYER LIFE
UNDERSTANDS GOD'S WORD
TRUSTS GOD
OBEYS GOD

Life Application

Write one new insight you have gained from this lesson concerning the Holy Spirit: _____

_____

_____

In what area of your life do you believe the Holy Spirit needs to be more in control? _____

_____

_____

_____

What will be the result when He is? _____

_____

_____

LESSON TWO

WHAT IS THE HOLY SPIRIT'S RELATIONSHIP WITH EVERY CHRISTIAN?

Introduction

OBJECTIVE: To realize the necessity of being filled with the Holy Spirit in order to live the Christian life.

TO MEMORIZE: Ephesians 5:18.

TO READ: Romans 12:1-8; 1 Corinthians 2.

Bible Study

A. *The work of the Holy Spirit*

   1. When you become a Christian (i.e., at the time of your spiritual birth), the Holy Spirit does a number of things for and in you. What are they?

     John 3:5 _____

     1 Corinthians 3:16 _____

     Ephesians 4:30 _____

     1 Corinthians 12:13 _____

     2 Corinthians 5:5 _____

   2. Explain in your own words what the Holy Spirit does for the Christian according to:

     Romans 8:16 _____

     _____

     Romans 8:26, 27 _____

     _____

B. *The results of being filled with the Holy Spirit*

   1. Can a person be a Christian and not have the Holy Spirit dwelling in Him (Romans 8:9)? Explain. _____

     _____

2. What is the main reason to be filled with the Spirit (Acts 1:8; 4:29, 31)? _____

_____

3. What work of the Holy Spirit is necessary for success-ful Christian living and service (Ephesians 5:18)? _____

_____

Life Application

Fill in the chart below:

"How I viewed the Holy Spirit in the past"	"How I view Him now"

Do you really desire to be filled with the Holy Spirit? _YES_

Why? _____

_____

_____

LESSON THREE

WHY ARE SO FEW CHRISTIANS FILLED WITH THE HOLY SPIRIT?

Introduction

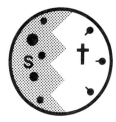

OBJECTIVE: To understand the barriers to a Spirit-filled life.

TO MEMORIZE: 1 John 2:15-17.

TO READ: Galatians 5 and 6; Acts 5:1-11.

Bible Study

A. *The heart's battlefield*

   1. How does Paul describe himself in Romans 7:19-24?

     _____

     _____

     What kind of feeling does that description arouse in you?

     _____

   2. State in your own words why there are so many unhappy

     Christians, according to Galatians 5:16, 17. _____

     _____

B. *Why the battle is often lost*

   1. Read the following Scriptures and state what you think they teach are the reasons so few Christians are filled with the Holy Spirit.

     Psalm 119:105   _____

     Proverbs 16:18   _____

     Proverbs 29:25   _____

     Luke 9:26   _____

   2. What is another thing that will put a block between you and the Lord and keep you from being filled with the

     Spirit (Psalm 66:18)? _____

     _____

What about 1 John 2:15-17? _____

3. Lack of trust in God also will keep you from being filled with the Holy Spirit. Read John 3:16 again. Do you feel that *you* could trust a God like this? _____

Why? (Romans 8:32 and 1 John 3:16 can help you with your answer.) _____

_____

_____

Basically, the reason most Christians are not filled with the Holy Spirit is that they are *unwilling to surrender their wills to God.*

- LEGALISTIC ATTITUDE
- IMPURE THOUGHTS
- JEALOUSY
- GUILT
- WORRY
- DISCOURAGEMENT
- CRITICAL SPIRIT
- FRUSTATION
- AIMLESSNESS

- IGNORANCE OF HIS SPIRITUAL HERITAGE
- UNBELIEF
- DISOBEDIENCE
- LOSS OF LOVE FOR GOD AND FOR OTHERS
- POOR PRAYER
- NO DESIRE FOR BIBLE STUDY

Life Application

List any barriers you are aware of now between yourself and God. _____

_____

Prayerfully consider, then answer this question:

"Am *I* willing to surrender my will to God?" _____

_____

_____

LESSON FOUR

HOW CAN A CHRISTIAN BE FILLED WITH THE HOLY SPIRIT?

Introduction

OBJECTIVE: To personally appropriate the filling of the Holy Spirit.

TO MEMORIZE: Romans 12:1, 2; 1 John 5:14, 15.

TO READ: Acts 6:8 - 7:60.

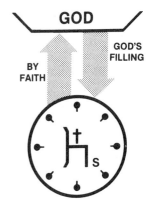

YOUR LOVE FOR CHRIST

A desire to serve Him and help others find Him should be your motive for being filled with the Holy Spirit. This lesson should not be completed until the entire article, "You Shall Receive Power," starting on page 127 has been studied carefully.

Bible Study

A. *What you must know*

1. What is the admonition found in Ephesians 5:18? _____

_____

2. Why do you need to be filled with the Spirit?

Galatians 5:22, 23 _____

Acts 1:8 _____

The fruit of the Spirit is never an end in itself, but only a means to the end that we win men and women to Christ, which in turn will bring glory and honor to Him (John 15:8).

B. *The one thing you must feel*

What is one prerequisite to being filled with the Spirit, according to Matthew 5:6? _____

_____

C. *What you must do*

1. If your desire to be filled with the Spirit is sincere, what will you do now (Romans 12:1, 2)? _____

   _____

   This means there can be no unconfessed sin in your life. The Holy Spirit cannot fill an unclean vessel. He waits to fill you with His power. Do not resist Him any longer.

2. How then are you filled with the Holy Spirit (Matthew 7:7-11; John 7:37)? _____

3. Will the Holy Spirit fill you if you ask Him? _____
   How do you know (1 John 5:14, 15)? _____

Life Application

You can be filled with the Holy Spirit only by faith. However, prayer is one way of expressing your faith. If you truly desire to be filled with the Holy Spirit, you can pray this prayer now:

"Dear Father, I need You. I acknowledge that I have been in control of my life; and that, as a result, I have sinned against You. I thank You that You have forgiven my sins through Christ's death on the cross for me. I now invite Christ to take control of the throne of my life. Fill me with the Holy Spirit as You commanded me to be filled, and as You promised in Your Word that You would do if I asked in faith. I pray this in the name of Jesus. As an expression of my faith, I now thank You for taking control of my life and for filling me with the Holy Spirit."

What must you do when you have asked Him to fill you (Hebrews 11:6)? _____

If you have asked the Holy Spirit to fill you, *thank Him.* God is dependable; His Word is true. If you are sincere, He has filled you. What should be your attitude from this day forward (1 Thessalonians 5:18)? _____

Date of filling _____

Your comments: _____

_____

_____

LESSON FIVE

HOW CAN A CHRISTIAN KNOW WHEN HE IS FILLED, AND WHAT ARE THE RESULTS OF BEING FILLED WITH THE SPIRIT?

Introduction

OBJECTIVE: To experience assurance of the filling of the Holy Spirit.

TO MEMORIZE: Galatians 5:22, 23.

TO READ: Galatians 5:16-26.

Did you sincerely follow the steps outlined in Lesson Four? Did you ask the Holy Spirit to fill you? If you did not, Lessons Five and Six will not mean much to you. Go back to Lesson Four and ask God to work in your heart. If He has filled you, you will be anxious to proceed with Lessons Five and Six.

Bible Study

A. *Results of the Spirit-filled life*

1. What will the Holy Spirit demonstrate in and through your life, as a result of His filling you (Galatians 5:22, 23)?

   _____

   Which specific fruit of the Spirit are you most in need of?

   _____

2. Read Acts 1:8. How do you see this power evidenced in your life? _____

   How does John 15:16 apply to you today? _____

   _____

3. How do you identify with 1 Corinthians 12:1-11 and Ephesians 4:11? _____

   _____

4. What mannerisms, language, activities and inconsistencies in your life do you feel are hindering the Holy Spirit's

development of His fruit, power and gifts in you? _____
_____

5. What happens as we are occupied with Christ and allow the Holy Spirit to work in us (2 Corinthians 3:18)? _____
_____

B. *Facts, faith and feelings*

1. What is the primary way we know if we have been filled with the Spirit (1 John 5:14, 15)? _____
_____

2. When you asked to be filled with the Spirit, did you feel any different? _____

Do not depend upon feeling. The promise of God's Word, not our feelings, is our authority. The Christian lives by faith (trust) in the trustworthiness of God Himself and His Word. This train diagram illustrates the relationship between *fact* (God and His Word), *faith* (our trust in God and His Word) and *feeling* (the result of our faith and obedience) (John 14:21).

The train will run with or without the caboose. However, it would be futile to attempt to pull the train by the caboose. In the same way, we, as Christians, do not depend upon feelings or emotions, but we place our faith (trust) in the trustworthiness of God and the promise of His Word.

Life Application

Though you may not be aware of change immediately, with the passing of time there should be some evidence of your being filled with the Spirit. Ask yourself these questions now and in the future from time to time:

1. Do you have a greater love for Christ? _____
2. Do you have a greater love for God's Word? _____
3. Are you more concerned for those who do not know Christ as Savior? _____
4. Are you experiencing a greater boldness, liberty and power in witnessing? _____

If you can answer "yes" truthfully to these questions, you undoubtedly are filled with the Spirit.

What does that knowledge mean to you now? _____

_____

_____

If your answer was "no" to any of those four questions, what do you suppose that indicates? _____

_____

_____

Do you think a person can be filled with the Holy Spirit and not be aware of it? _____ Explain. _____

_____

_____

_____

LESSON SIX

HOW CAN A CHRISTIAN CONTINUE TO BE FILLED WITH THE HOLY SPIRIT?

Introduction

OBJECTIVE: To make the Spirit-filled life a moment-by-moment reality.

TO MEMORIZE: John 14:21 or John 15:10.

TO READ: Acts 10.

Bible Study

How to be filled continually

Read Ephesians 5:18. In the original Greek, "be filled" means "keep on being filled constantly and continually."

1. In prayer you must not only pray for yourself, but _____ _____ (Ephesians 6:18 and 1 Samuel 12:23). What person have you stopped praying for recently who still needs your prayers? _____

2. You must _____ daily (Acts 17:11). What does the Word of God do for you (Psalm 119:11)? _____

3. You must abide in Christ. How can you do that? (John 14:21 and John 15:10)? _____ Which two commandments do you think are the most important? _____ _____

4. Read Ephesians 4:25-32. How do you grieve the Holy Spirit? _____ _____

   Which commandment in that list do you need to pay

special attention to? _____

5. How can you get rid of sin in your life (1 John 1:9)? _____

_____

6. What do you think Romans 8:13 teaches that the Holy Spirit wants to do for you? _____

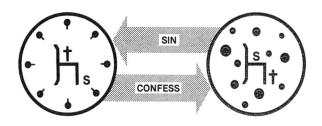

Life Application

The Spirit-filled life is an obedient and abiding life. It can be experienced daily as you:

Begin each day by asking God to cleanse your life, according to 1 John 1:9.

Present your body to the Holy Spirit according to Romans 12:1, 2 and ask Him to keep you filled with His power.

Ask the Holy Spirit to lead you to men who are lost. Be sensitive to His leading.

Expect others to come to Christ through your witness. Do not quench the Spirit by failing to respond.

Rejoice in all things, praising God even in adversity (1 Thessalonians 5:18; Romans 8:28).

1. What sin do you need to confess today? _____

_____

2. Have you realized today victory over a sin you confessed yesterday? _____

_____

LESSON SEVEN

RECAP

Review verses memorized.

Read: John 14:16-26; John 16:7-15.

Is the Holy Spirit a personality or an impersonal force? _____
_____ How do you know? _____
_____

What is the chief reason the Holy Spirit has come? _____
_____

What is the command of Ephesians 5:18? _____
_____

Name as many reasons as you can that Christians are not filled with the Holy Spirit. _____
_____
_____
_____
_____

What should be your motives for being filled with the Spirit?
_____

How can a Christian be filled with the Spirit? _____
_____

How do you know you are filled with the Holy Spirit? _____
_____

How can you continue to be filled with and to walk in the Spirit?
_____
_____
_____
_____